HIDDEN PICTURE LINE ONE COLOR COLORING BOOK

AUTHOR:
AENIGMATIS

First published 2021

Copyright @ 2021, Aenigmatis. All rights reserved.

No part of this publication may be reproduced in any material form (including photocopying or storing in any medium by electronic means and whether or not transiently or incidentally to some other use of this publication) without the written permission of the copyright holder.

ISBN-13: 9798737927059

WWW.AENIGMATIS.EU

HIDDEN PICTURE LINE IMAGES   3

- The hidden pictures are made from many closed lines
- Fill in all the closed lines with ink, paint or soft pencil, to reveal the picture
- Don't fill in any areas that are not within a closed line (open areas)
- Acrylic paint pens (water based paint markers) one with an extra fine tip (1mm) & one with a medium tip (3mm) are ideal for these pictures

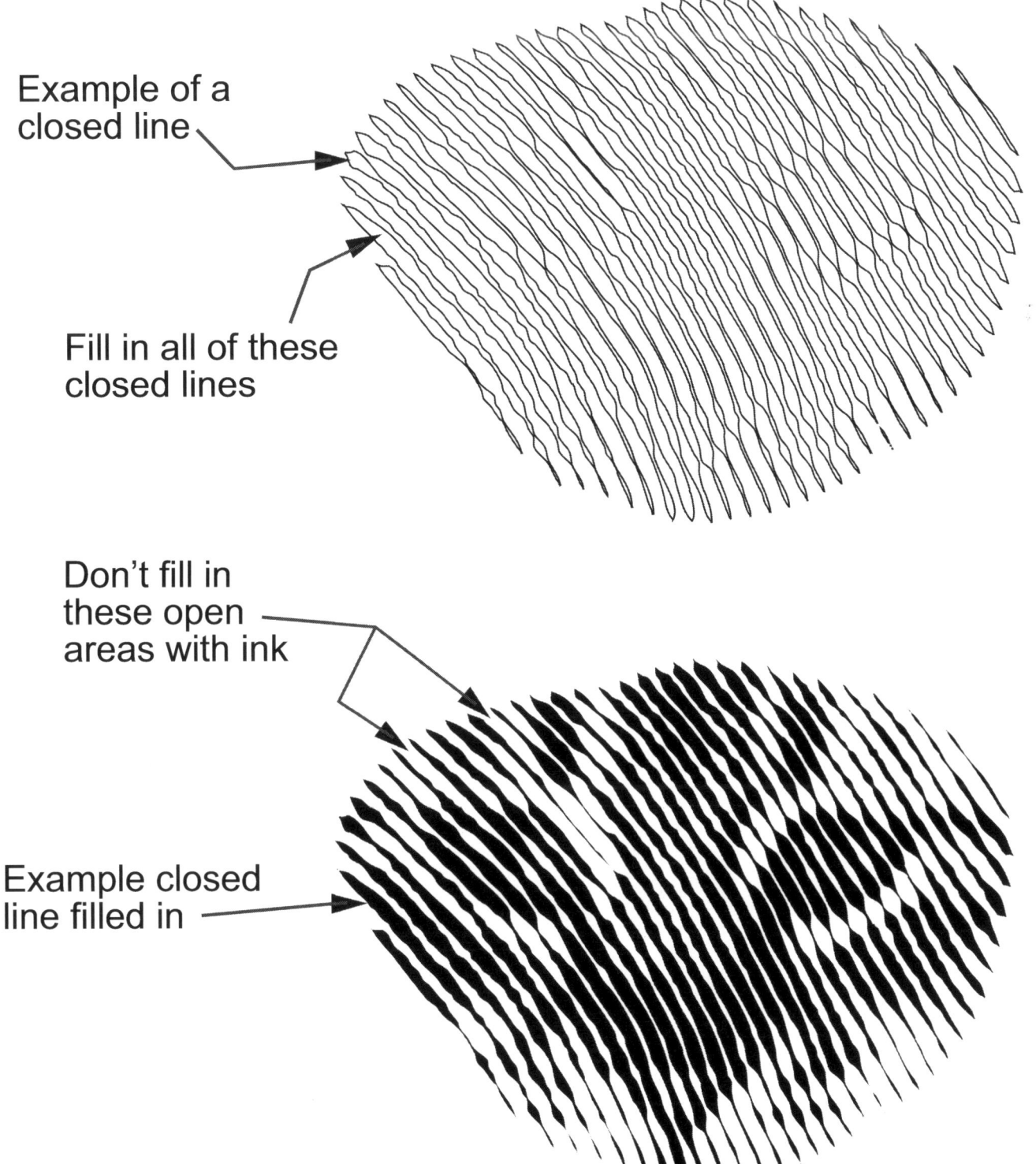

Example of a closed line

Fill in all of these closed lines

Don't fill in these open areas with ink

Example closed line filled in

4

6

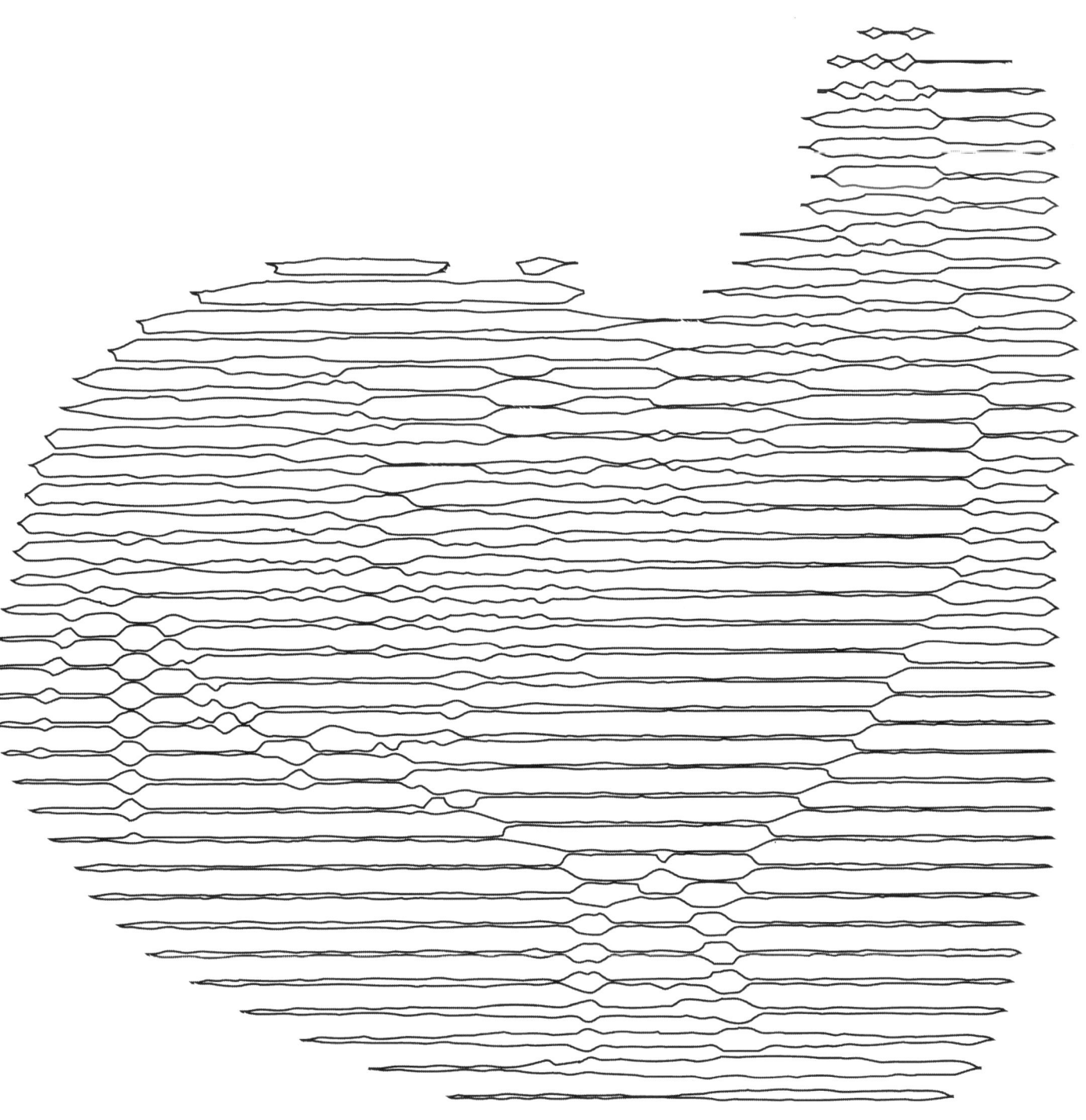

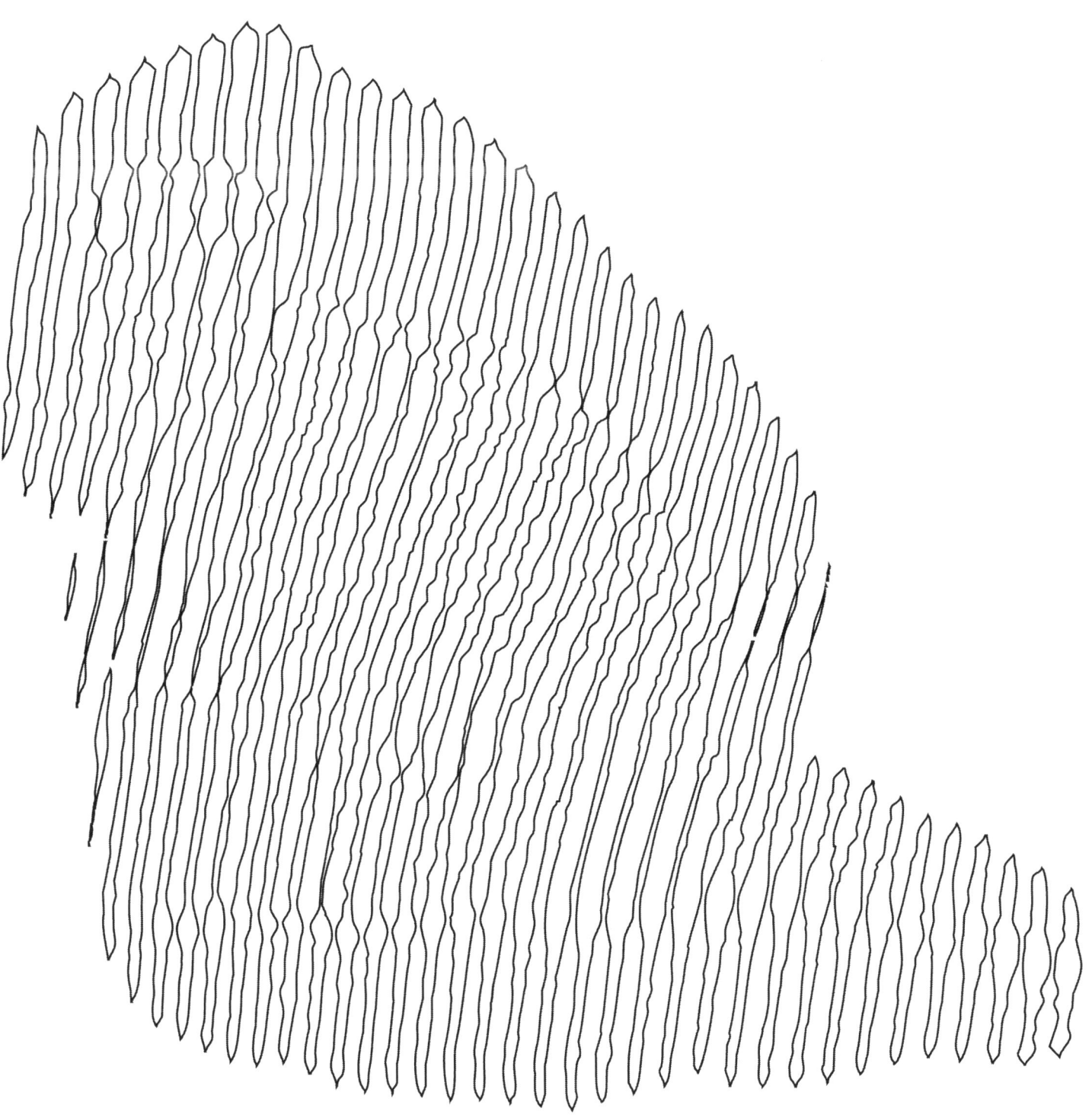

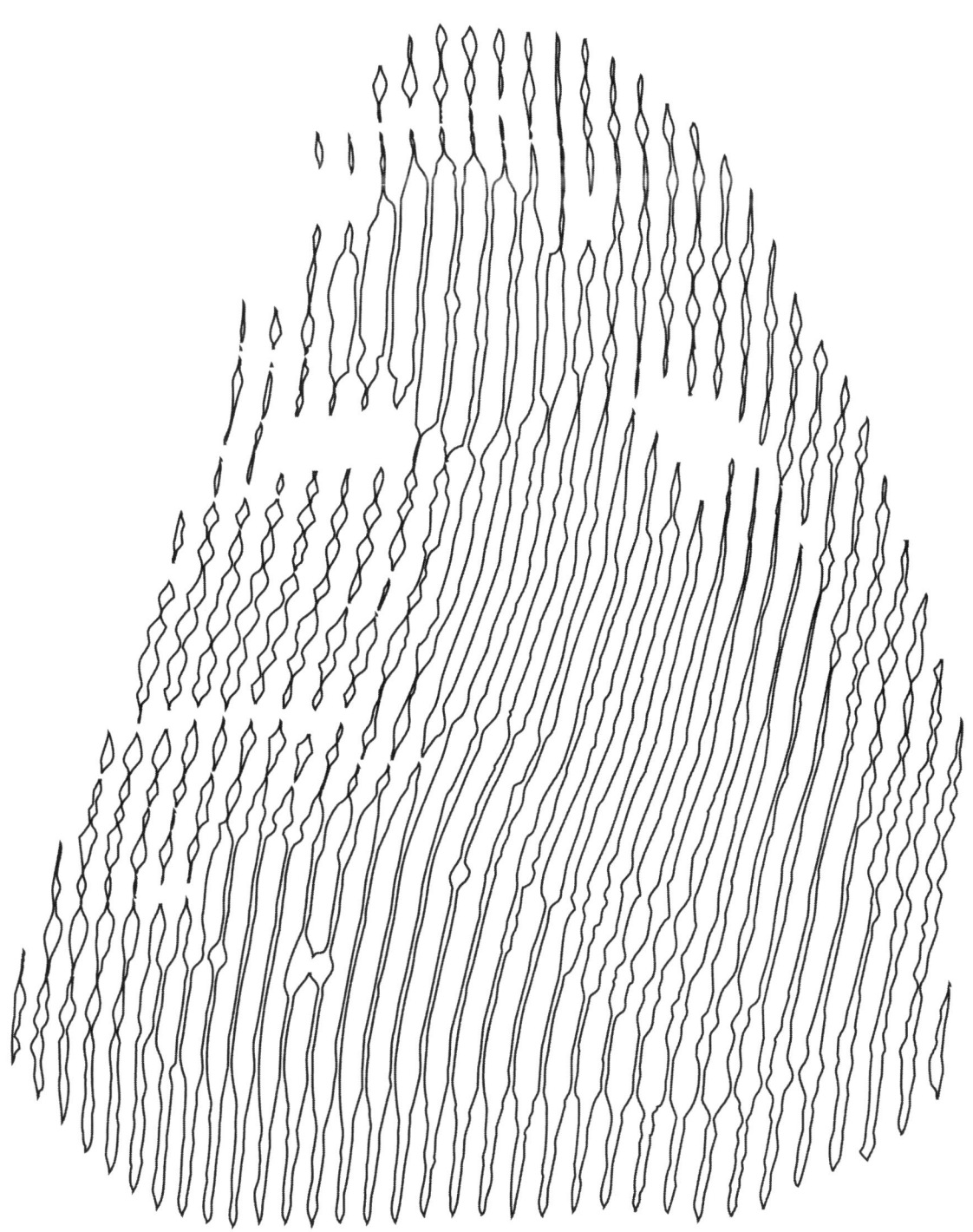

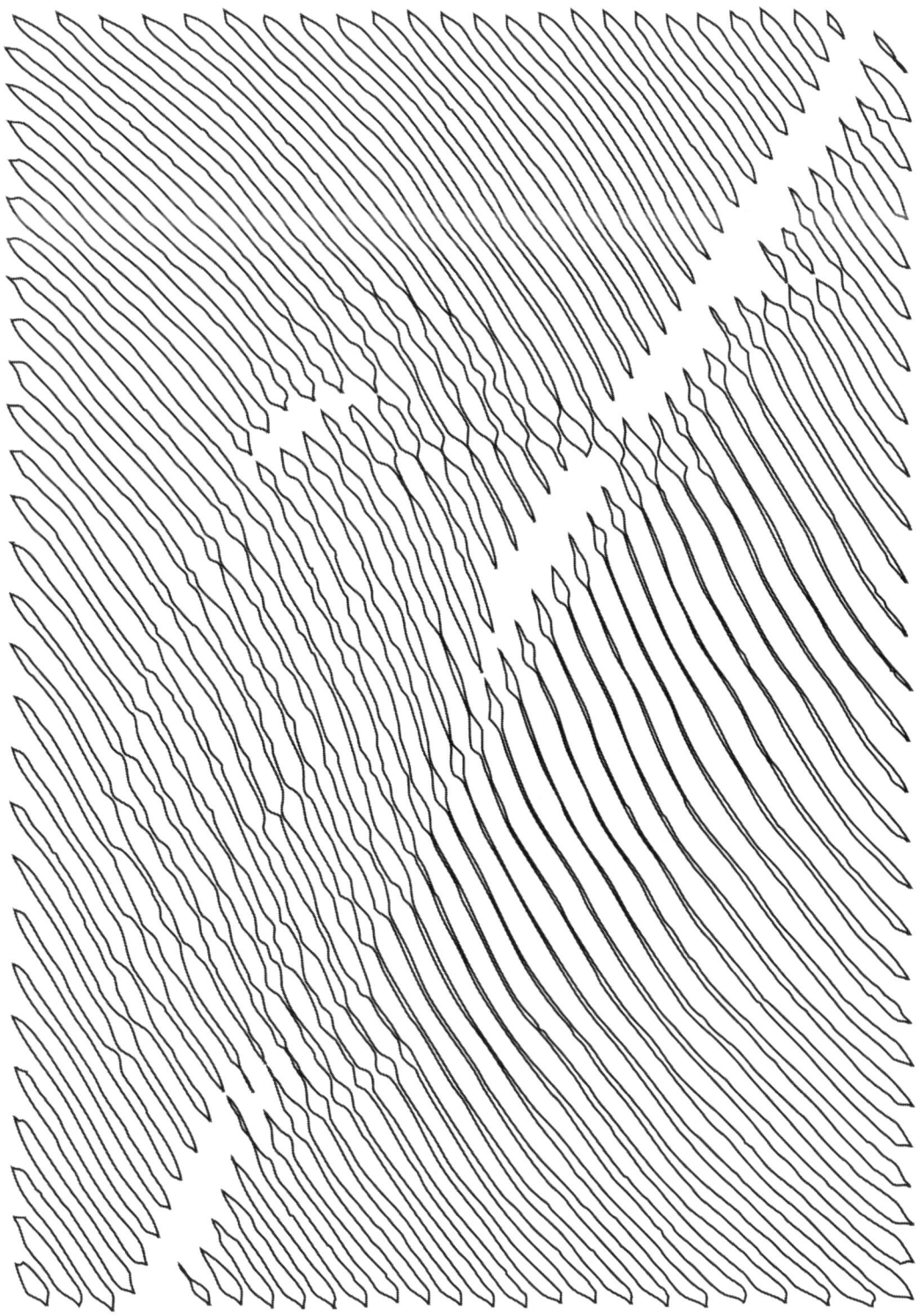

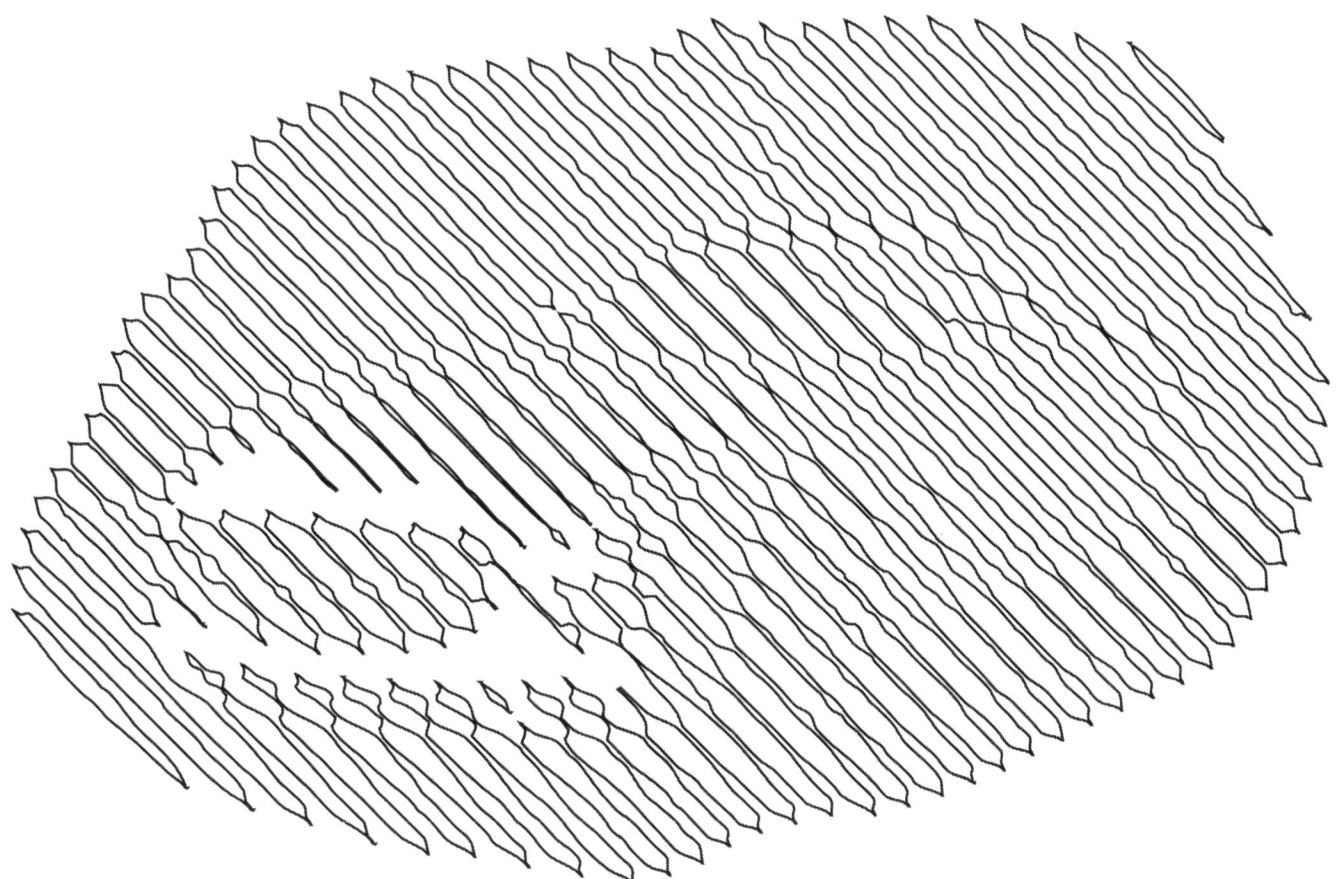

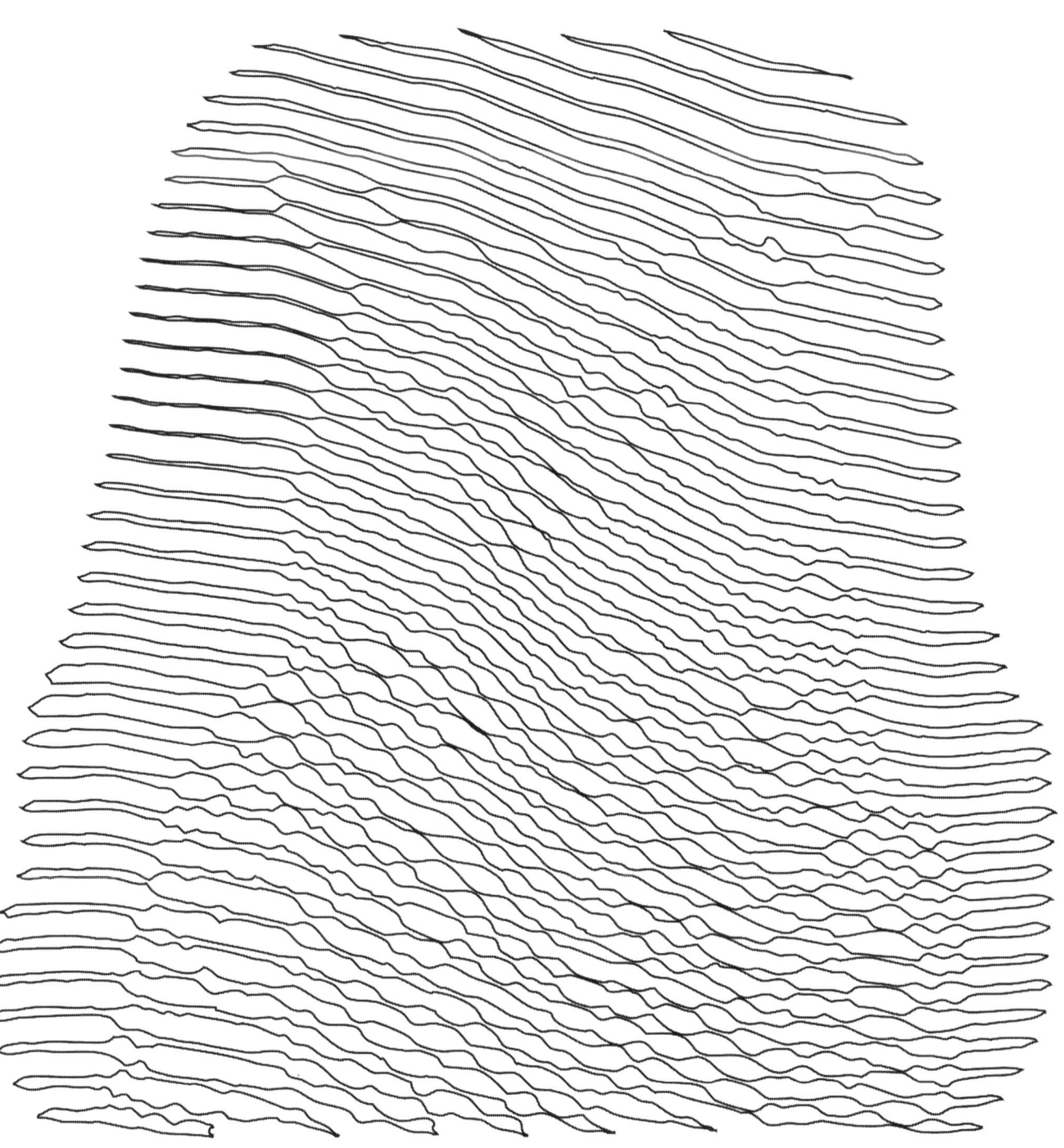

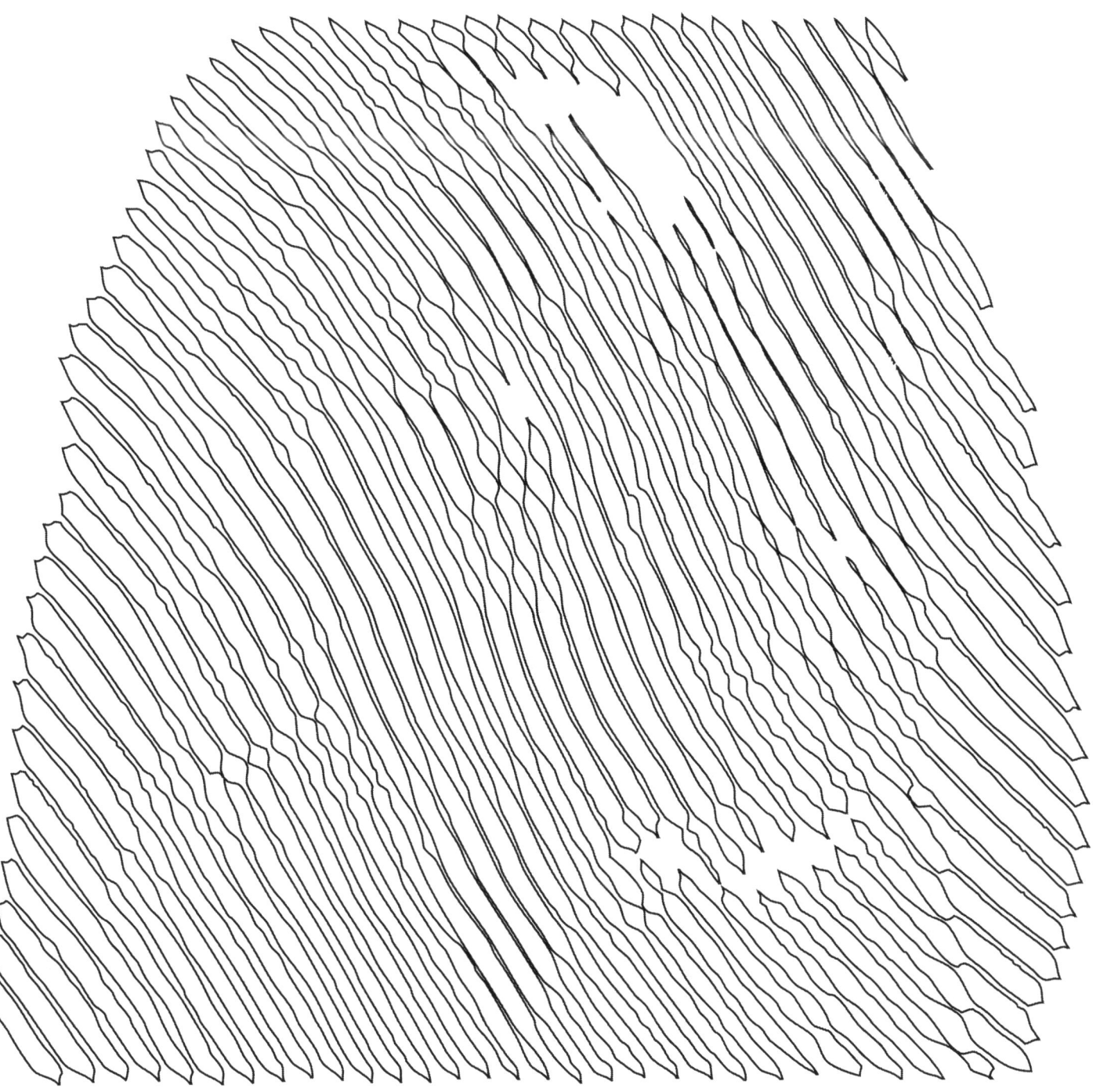

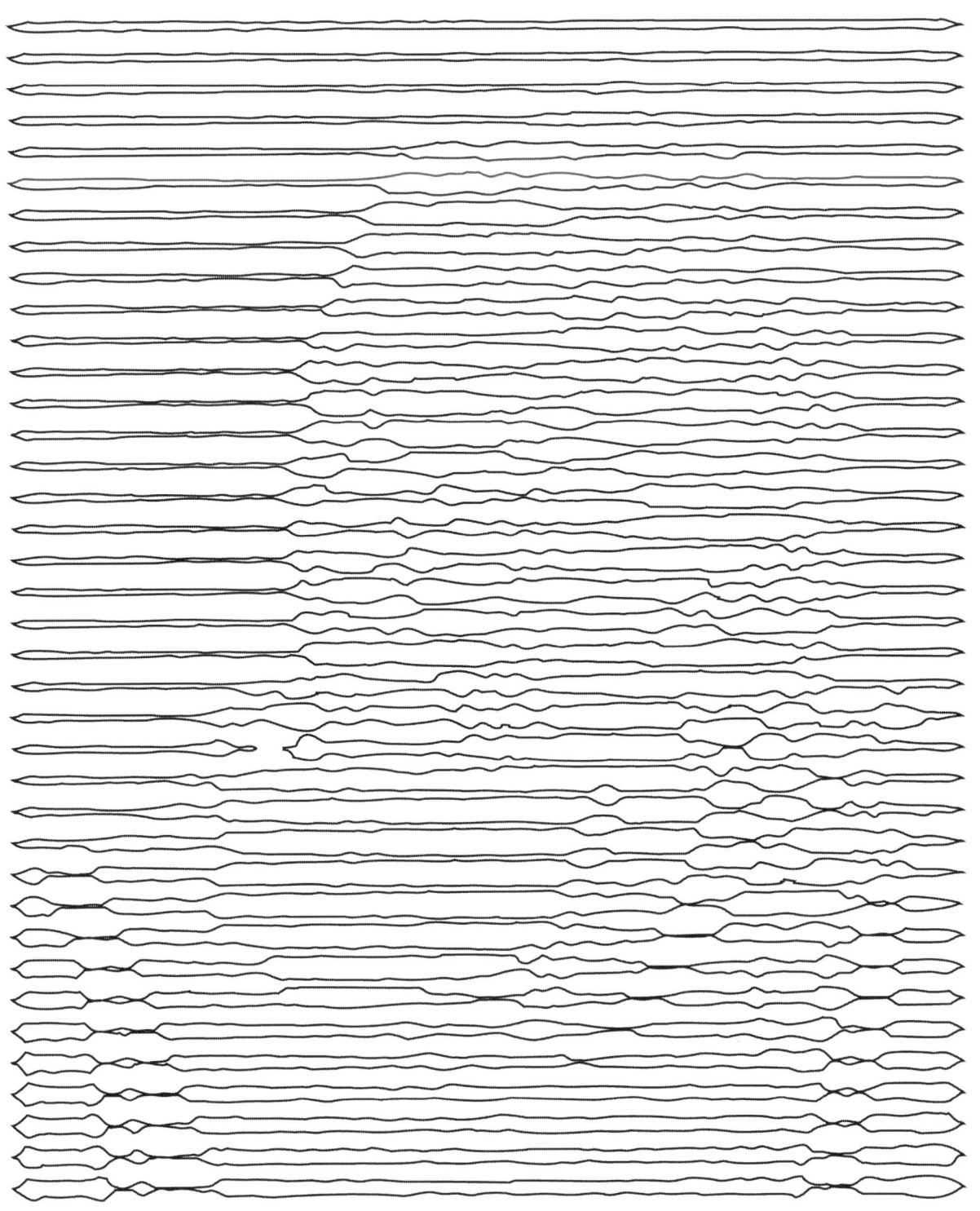

41

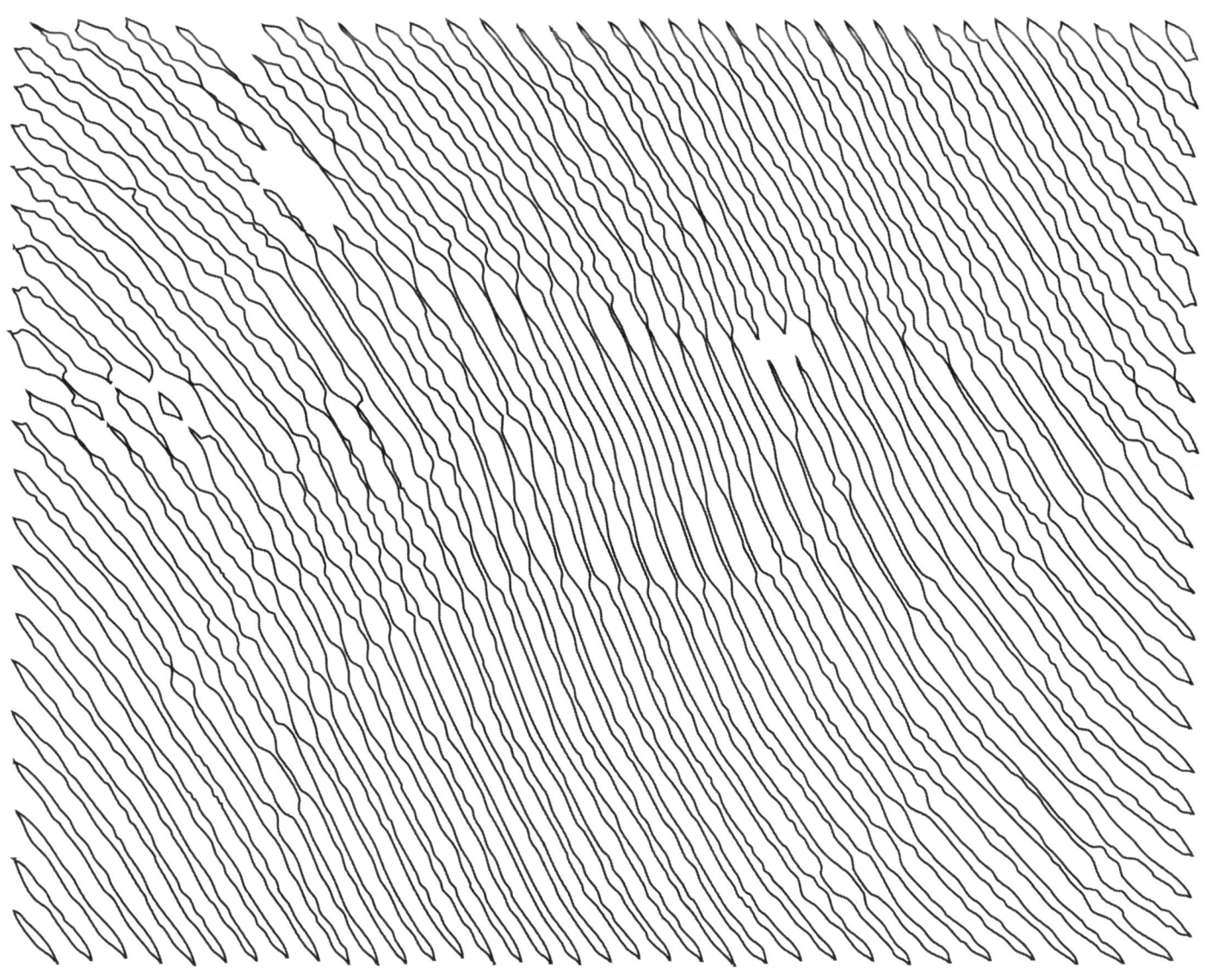

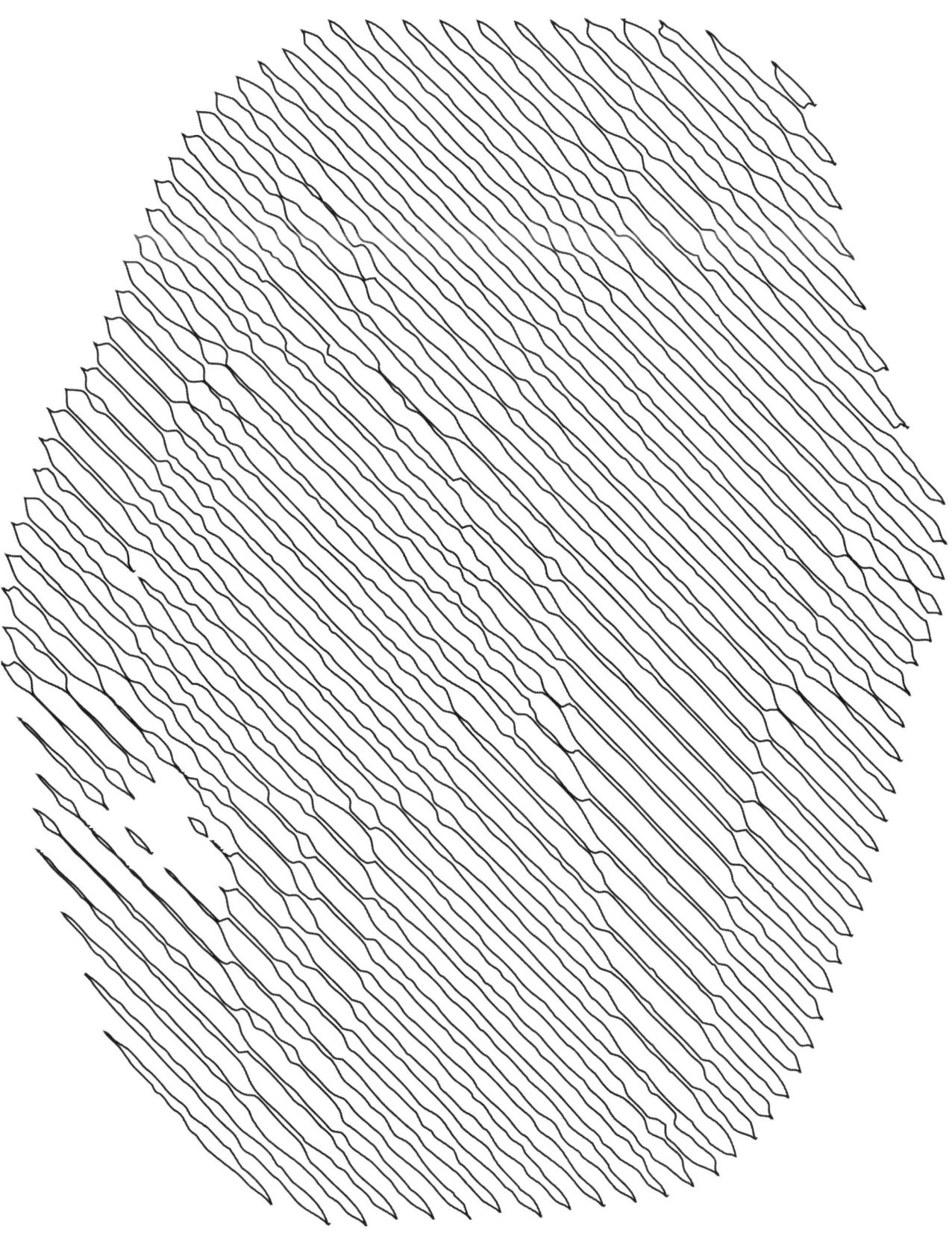

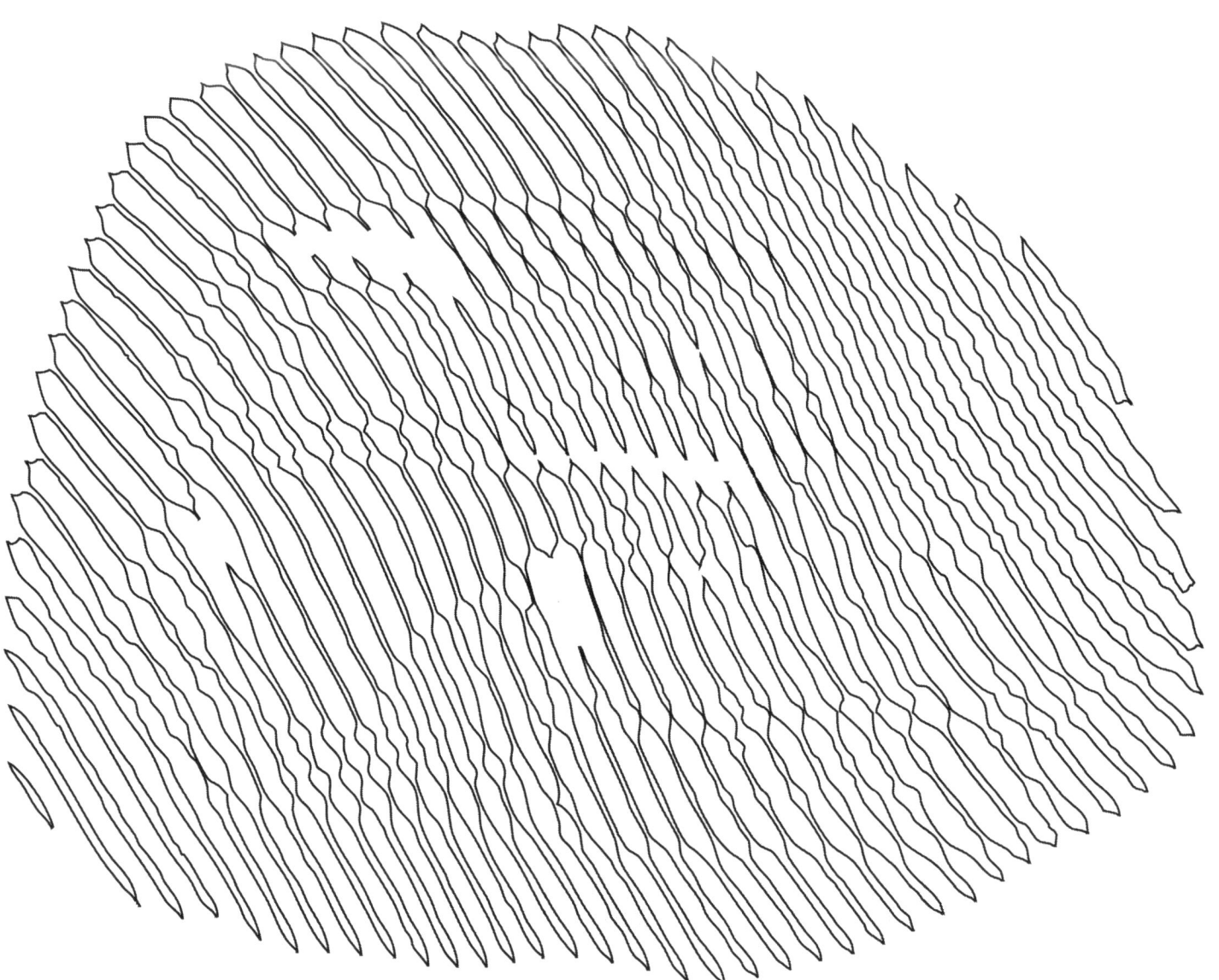

SOLUTIONS

PAGE 5

PAGE 7

PAGE 9

PAGE 11

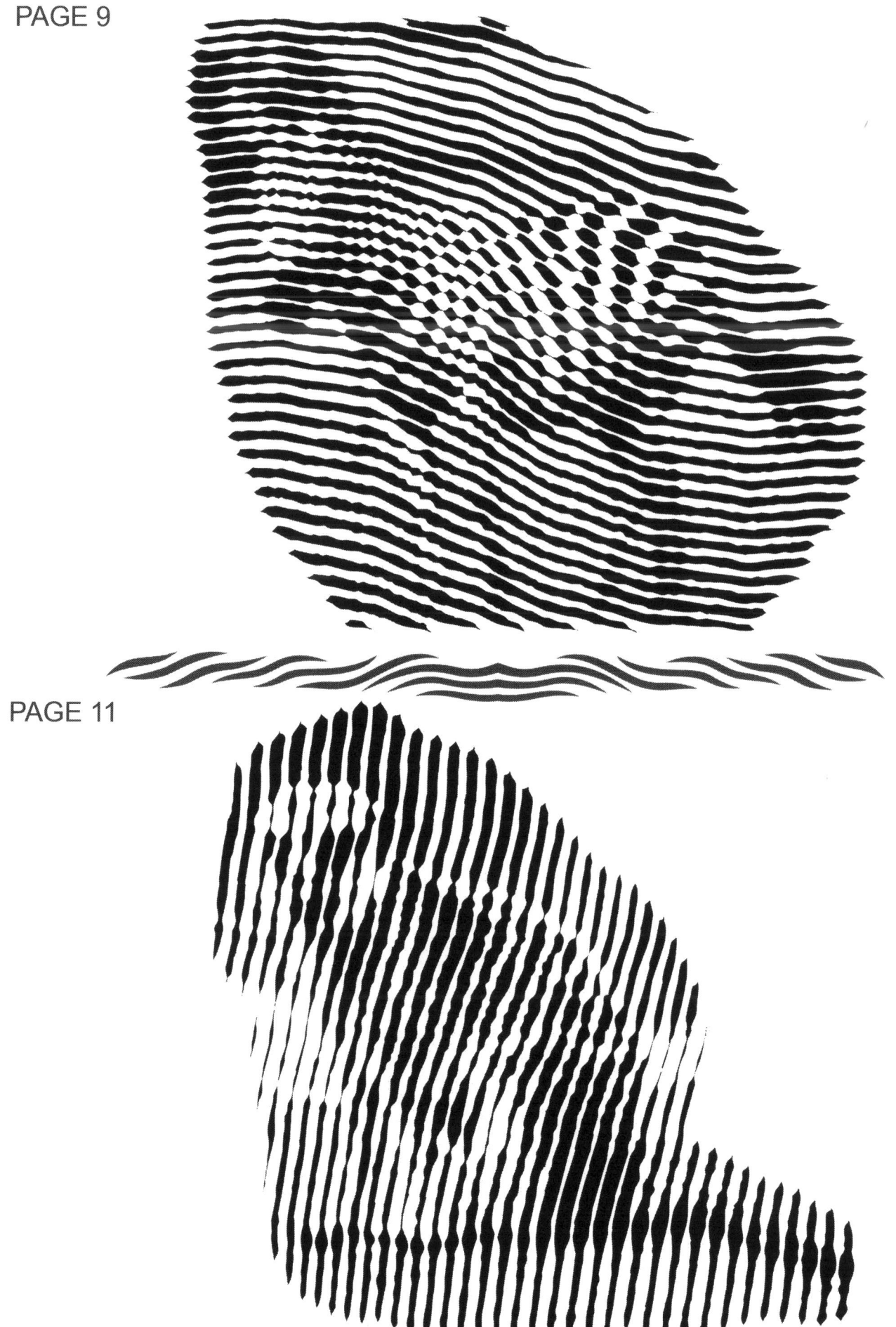

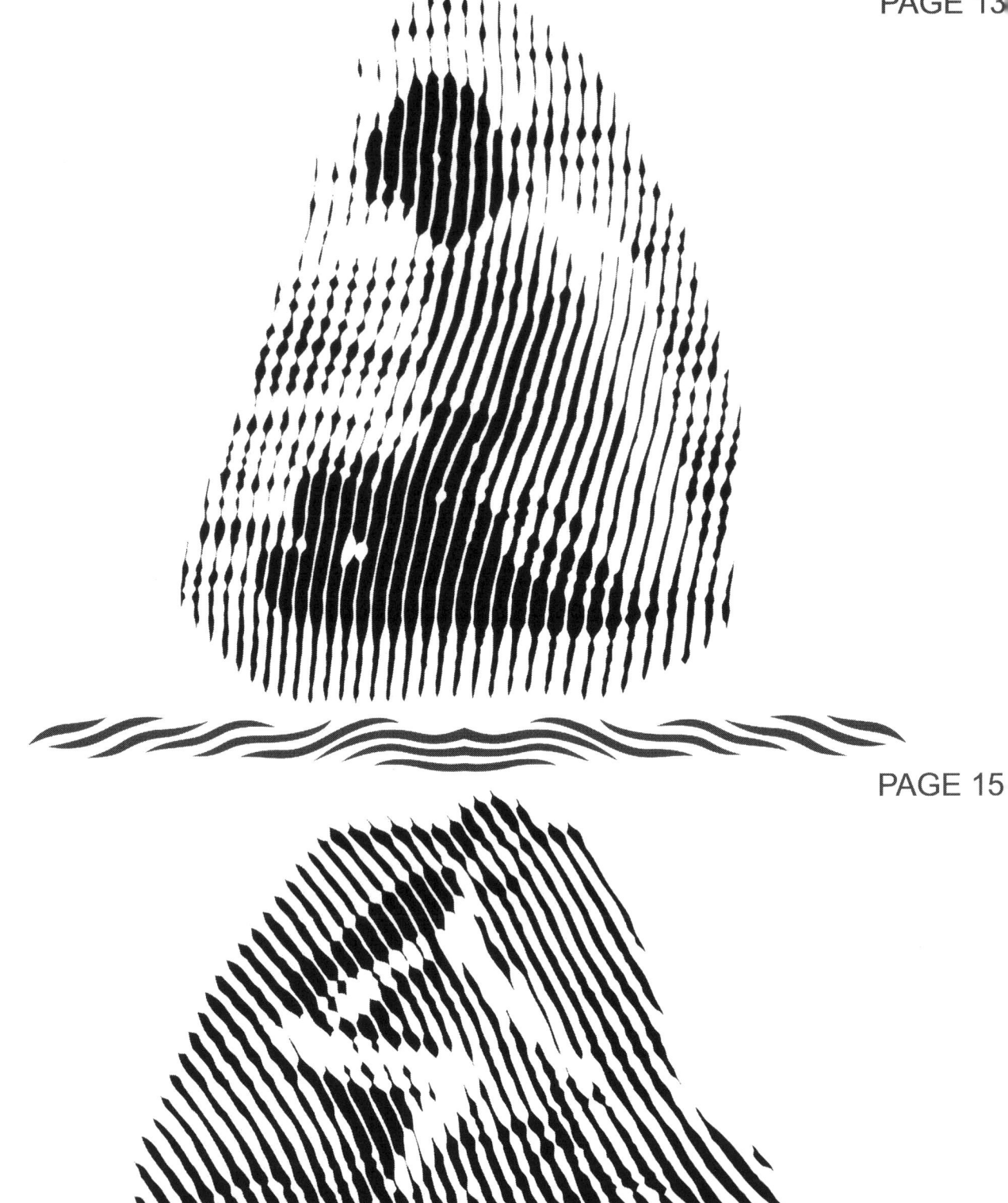

PAGE 17

PAGE 19

PAGE 21

PAGE 23

PAGE 25

PAGE 27

PAGE 33

PAGE 35

62

PAGE 37

PAGE 39

PAGE 41

PAGE 43

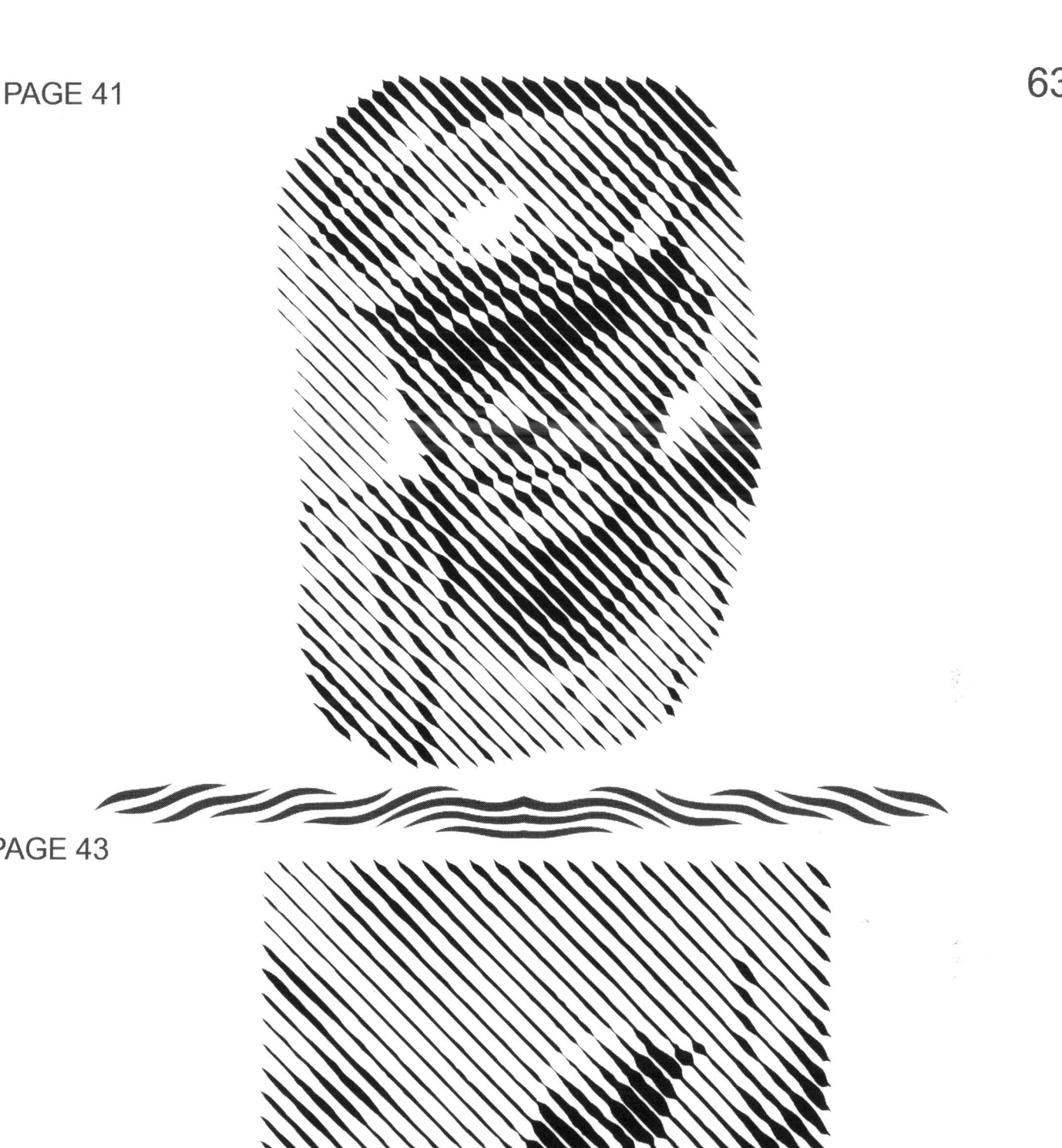

PAGE 45

PAGE 47

PAGE 49

PAGE 51

BONUS PUZZLES FROM AENIGMATIS BOOKS

ISBN-13 : 979-8722265302

ISBN-13 : 979-8558048438

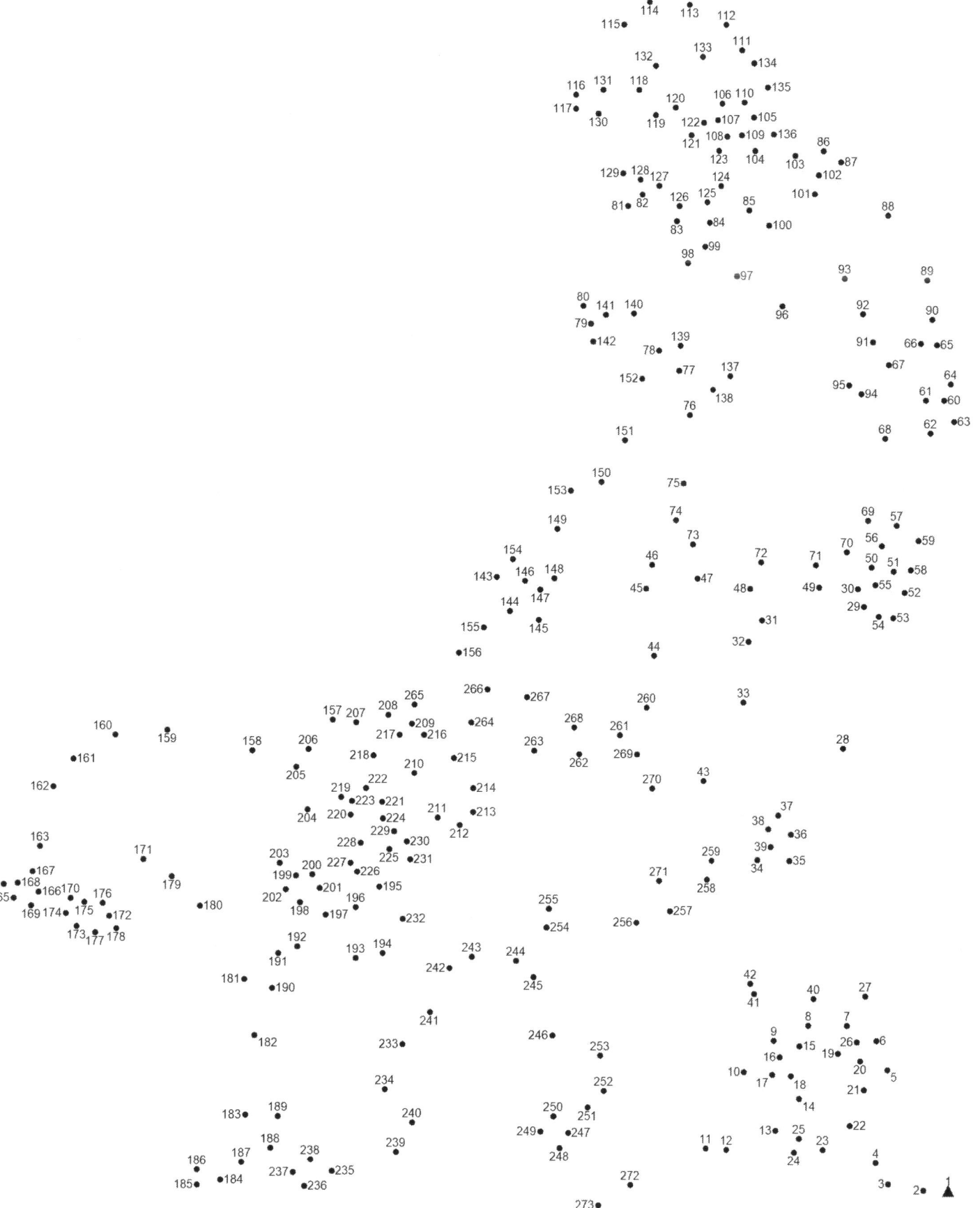

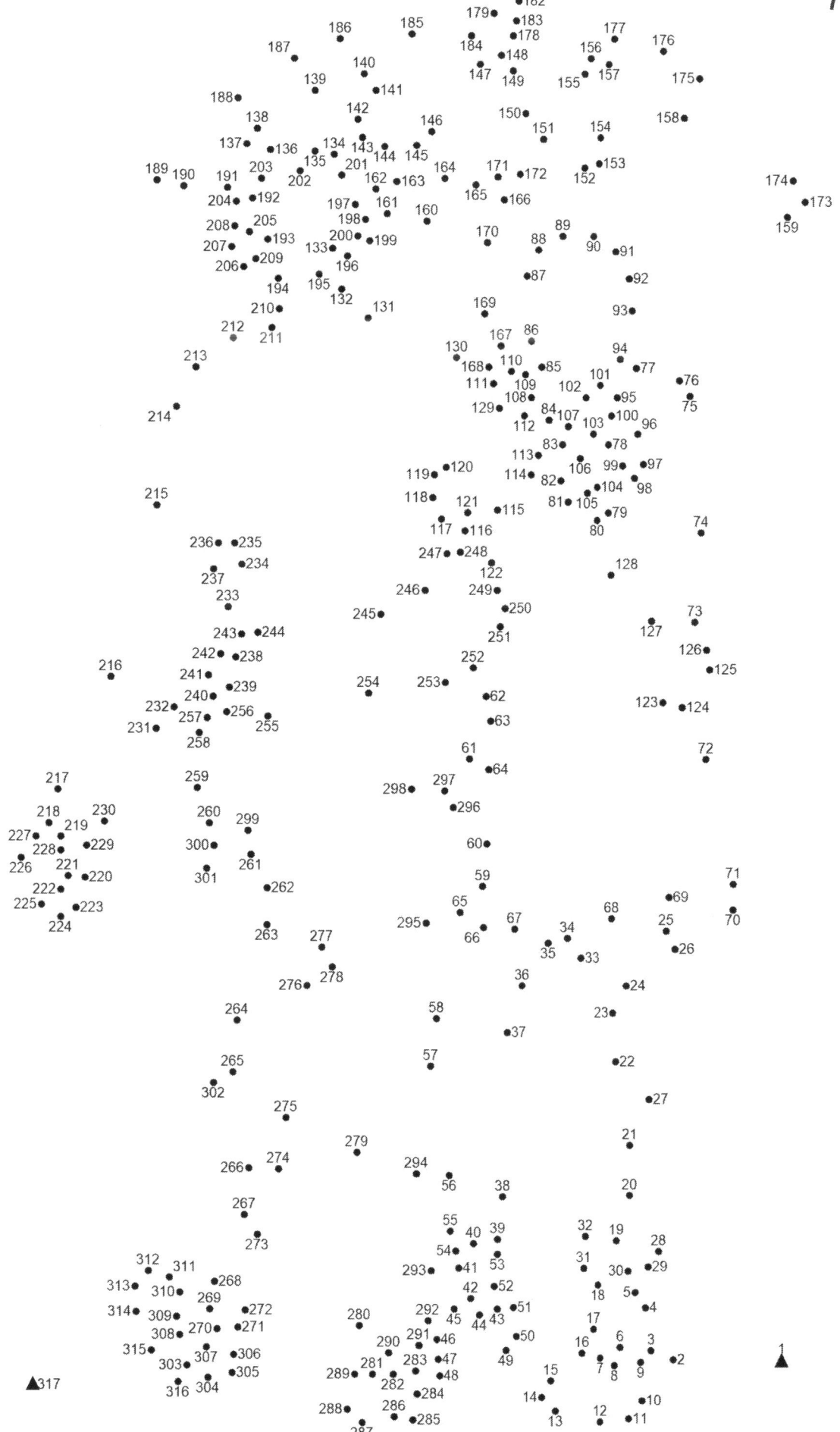

73

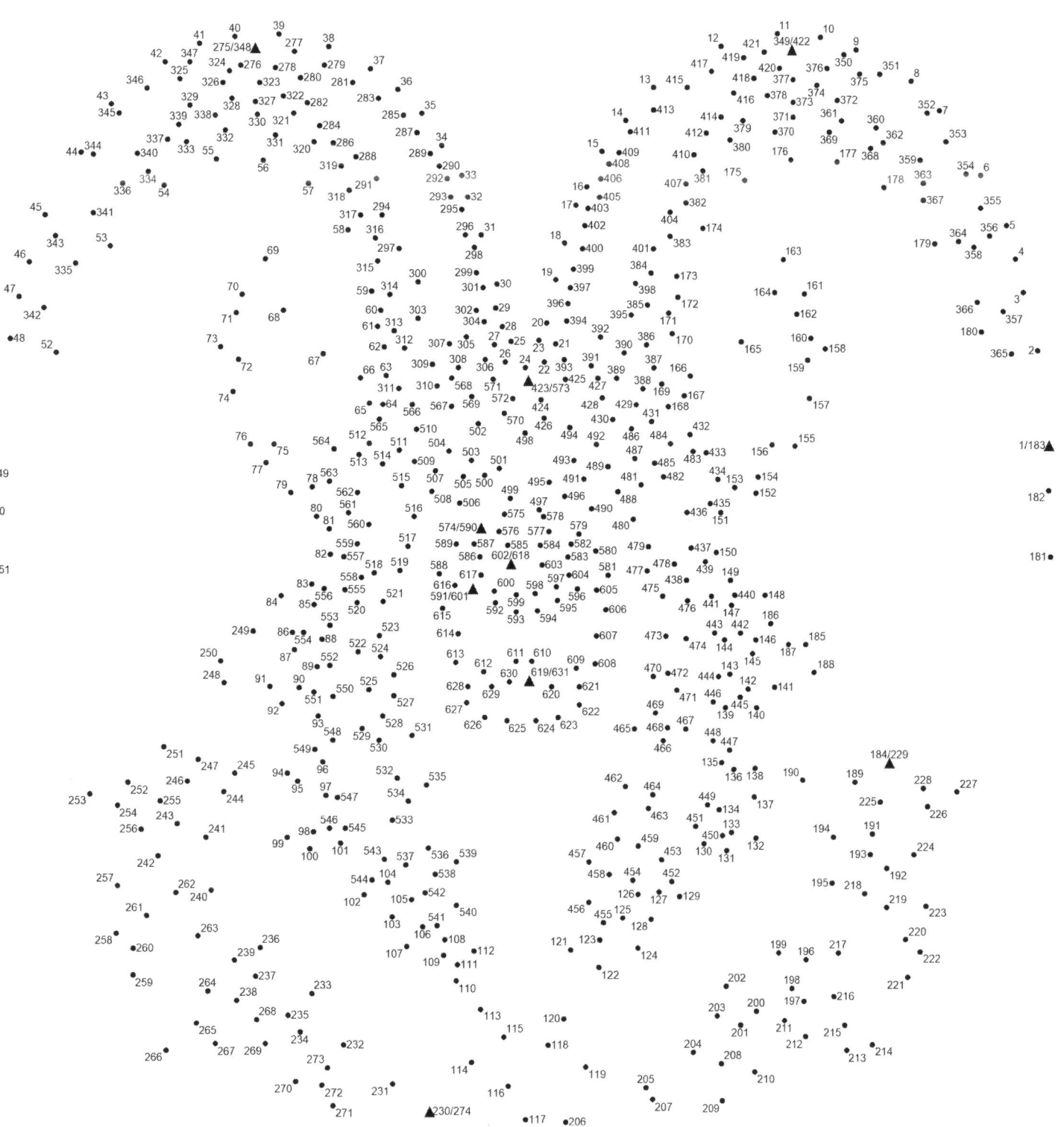

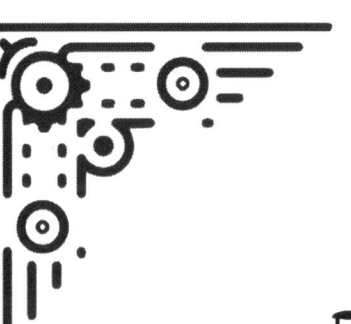

BONUS SOLUTIONS

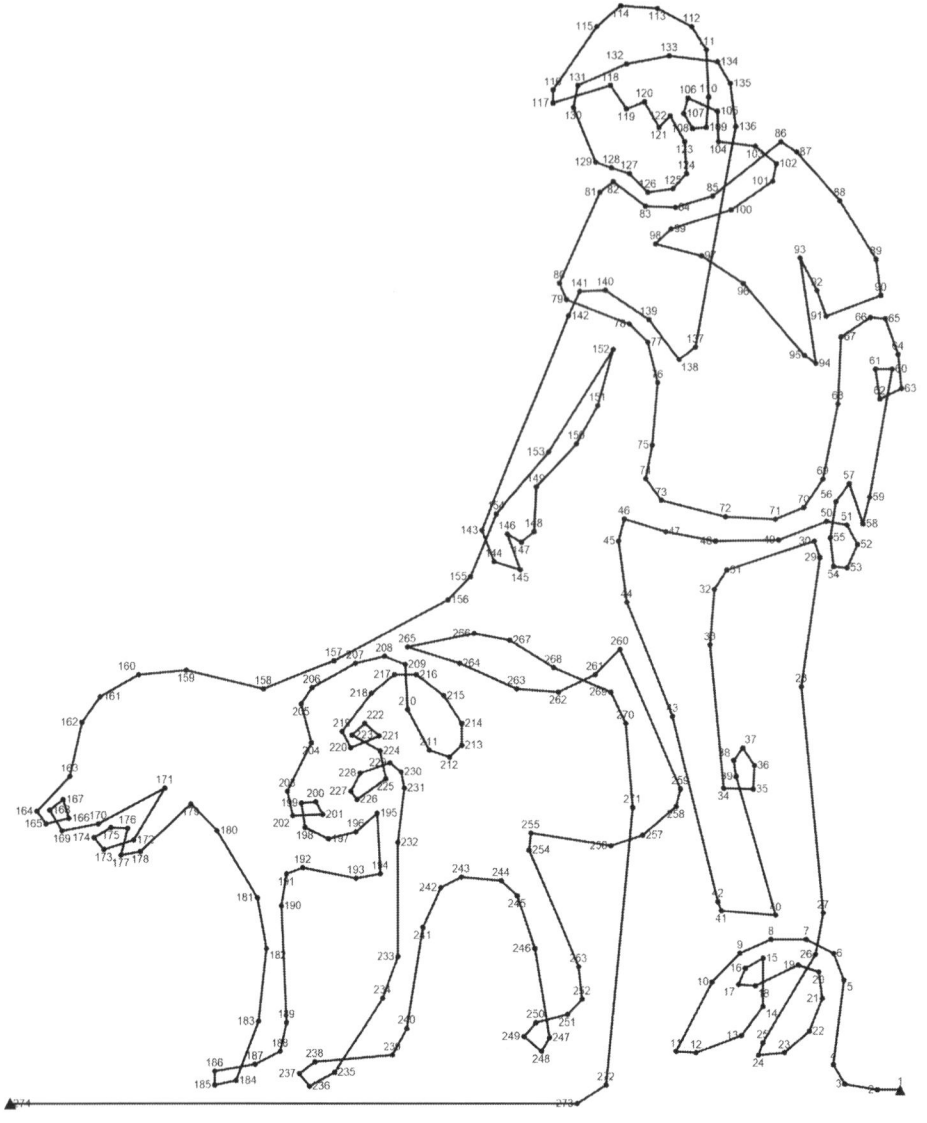

PAGE 71

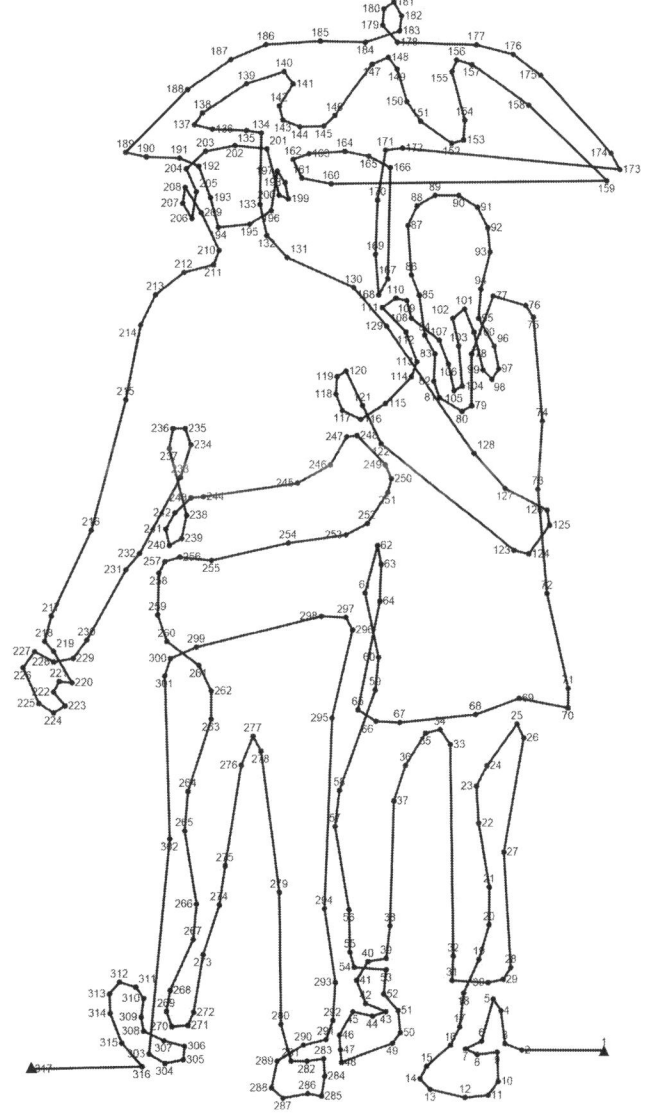

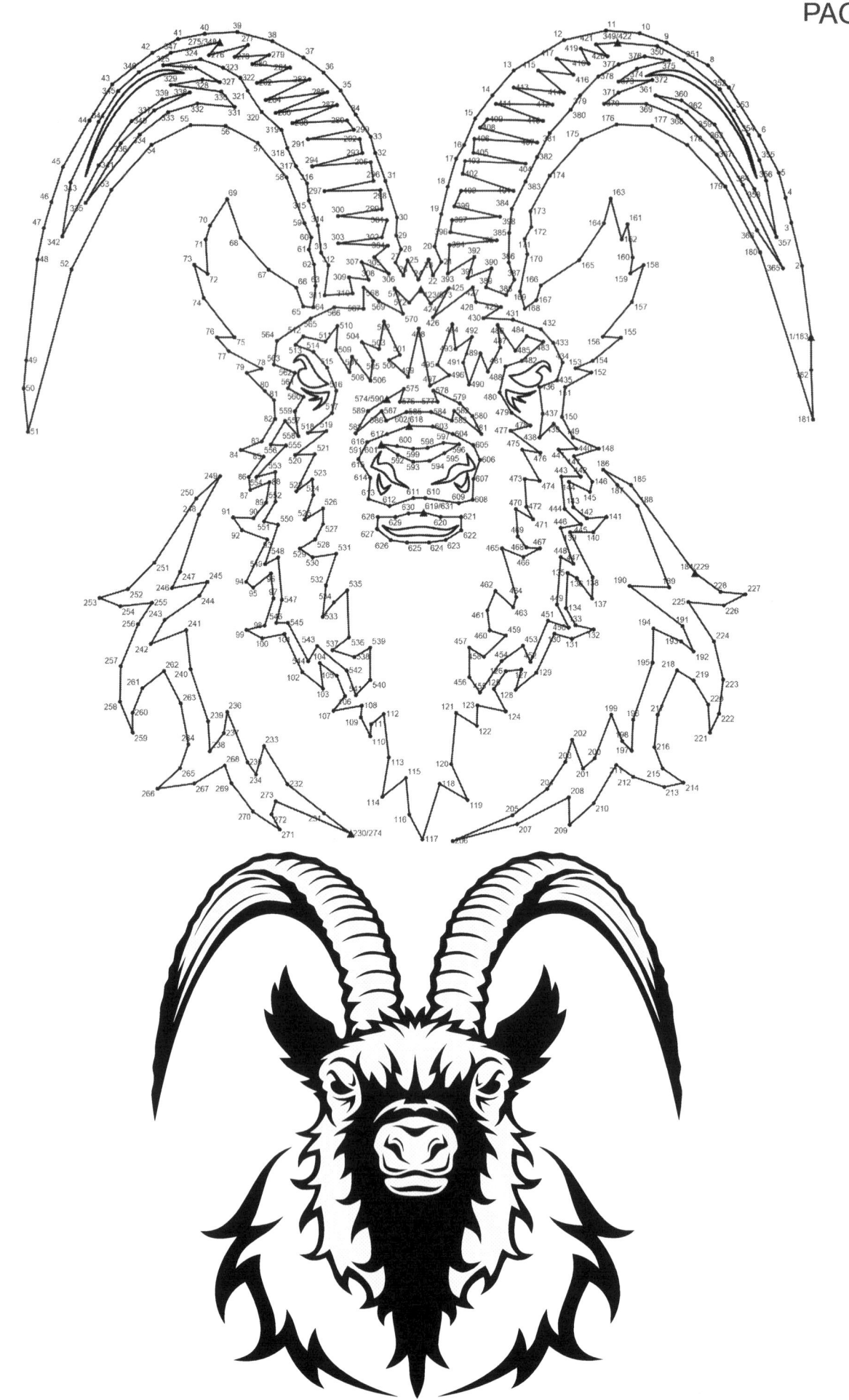

PAGE 75

81

Printed in Great Britain
by Amazon